W9-CMJ-322

A New True Book

GRAND CANYON

NATIONAL PARK

By David Petersen

CHILDRENS PRESS®

CHICAGO

The Grand Canyon from
the North Rim

Project Editor: Fran Dyra
Design: Margrit Fiddle

Library of Congress Cataloging-in-Publication Data

Petersen, David.
 Grand Canyon National Park / by David Petersen.
  p.   cm. — (A New true book)
 Includes index.
 Summary: Describes the formation of the remarkable
canyons in this national park in Arizona and discusses
other things to see and do there.
 ISBN 0-516-02197-4
  1. Grand Canyon National Park (Ariz.)—Juvenile
literature. [1. Grand Canyon National Park (Ariz.)
2. National parks and reserves.] I. Title.
F788.P48 1992
917.91′320453—dc20   92-11343
                                             CIP
                                              AC

PHOTO CREDITS

© Reinhard Brucker—6, 26 (bottom left), 27 (top left),
29 (right), 31 (center), 32 (right); Field Museum,
Chicago, 36 (bottom left), 38 (left); Meier Collection,
38 (right)

© Cameramann International, Ltd.—7, 14 (top), 20
(left), 41 (3 photos)

© Virginia R. Grimes—32 (left)

H. Armstrong Roberts—© M. Schneiders, Cover

© Jerry Hennen—26 (top left), 27 (bottom left), 31
(left), 33, 36 (top left)

© Jason Lauré—18

Photri—10 (left), 12

© Branson Reynolds—13, 14 (bottom), 17 (bottom),
25 (2 photos), 28 (right), 30 (left), 35 (left), 40 (right),
44 (right)

Root Resources—© James Blank, 4; © Ruth A. Smith,
9, 17 (top), 22

© James P. Rowan—39, 40 (left)

© Tom Schiltz—23 (right), 43

Bob and Ira Spring—11 (left)

Tom Stack & Associates—© Barbara von Hoffmann,
10 (right); © Tom Algire, 19; © Spencer Swanger, 21;
© Thomas Kitchin, 26 (right); © Larry Brock, 45 (left)

Valan—© Don McPhee, 2; © M. G. Kingshott, 20 (right),
42 (2 photos), © Robert C. Simpson, 23 (left); © John
Cancalosi, 27 (right), 36 (bottom right); © Stephen
Krasemann, 28 (left); © Aubrey Lang, 29 (left);
© Michael J. Johnson, 30 (right); © Jeff Foott, 44 (left)

Horizon Graphics—map, 4

Cover—Pima Point, Grand Canyon National Park

TABLE OF CONTENTS

GRAND
CANYON
NATIONAL
PARK

Colorado River

ARIZONA

The Grand Canyon is
in northwestern Arizona.

A HUGE HOLE IN THE GROUND

Have you heard about Grand Canyon National Park? It's in Arizona. And it's big—1,904 square miles (4,931 square kilometers).

Every year, millions of people go to see the Grand Canyon, a huge hole in the ground.

The Grand Canyon is 277 miles (446 kilometers) long, about 10 miles (16

The Sears Tower in Chicago, Illinois, is the tallest building in the world.

kilometers) across, and 1 mile (1.6 kilometers) deep.

Picture it this way: The tallest building in the world is the Sears Tower in Chicago, Illinois. It is 1,454 feet (443 meters) high. It would take four Sears Towers, stacked one on top of the other, to reach from the bottom to the top of the Grand Canyon!

The Colorado River flows through the bottom of the canyon. It's a big river, averaging 200 feet (61 meters) wide. But from the canyon's rim, you can barely see it way down at the bottom.

This view shows the Colorado River flowing through the Grand Canyon.

LONG AGO IN THE WEST

Long ago, before the Grand Canyon existed, the western United States was covered by a shallow sea.

Tons of silt—tiny particles of powdered sand and rock—were suspended in the water. Then the sea dried up, and all the silt settled to the bottom to form a thick layer of muck.

Later, a new sea came, bringing more silt. Over millions of years, many

seas came and went.
Thousands of layers of
sand and mud were
deposited in this way. Very
slowly, these mucky layers
hardened into rock.

Today, you can see
these rock layers exposed

Rock layers in the canyon walls were exposed by erosion.

Left: View from Yaki Point.
Above: Waterfalls in Saddle
Canyon, one of many side
canyons that branch off
from the Grand Canyon.

in the walls of the Grand
Canyon. Some of the
layers contain fossils of
sea creatures turned to
stone.

Because the bottom
layers were deposited first,
they are older than the top

Sunrise at the South Rim

layers. The oldest rocks at
the Grand Canyon are
about two billion years old.
That's nearly half as old
as the Earth itself!

But how was the Grand
Canyon formed?

The Grand Canyon was
cut by running water. For

11

six million years, the Colorado River has been slowly rubbing away at the rock layers. This slow wearing away is called erosion. Even today, the Colorado River continues to erode the Grand Canyon.

The Colorado River winds through the canyon.

Visitors gather on the rim to see the canyon.

VISITING THE GRAND CANYON

The Grand Canyon is one of the wonders of the world. People come from many countries to see it. On any day there, you may hear people speaking German, Japanese,

13

Views from Maricopa Point (above) and Yavapai Point (below)

Spanish, English, and other languages.

Most visitors head for the scenic viewpoints along the canyon rims. Some favorite viewpoints are Powell, Grandview, Maricopa, Yavapai, and Mohave. From each of these high places, you can see for miles down the canyon.

But there is more to do at the Grand Canyon than just look at it.

There are two main visitor areas at Grand Canyon National Park. The South Rim is the most popular. In summer, it gets crowded with cars. Smart visitors park their cars and get around on foot or ride bicycles. Or they take the free shuttle bus.

At Grand Canyon Village, on the South Rim, are hotels, restaurants, gift shops, museums, and campgrounds. From Grand

Visitors can stay at lodges in Grand Canyon Village (above) and visit Hopi House (below).

Hiking trails give visitors a close-up view of the canyon.

Canyon Village you can hike along the Canyon Rim Nature Trail.

Fewer people go to the North Rim of the Grand Canyon. The North Rim is about 1,000 feet (305 meters) higher than the South Rim. It gets more rain and snow, and it is cooler and greener.

Grand Canyon National Park has many hiking trails. The two most

The North Rim in the light of the late-afternoon sun

Bright Angel Lodge (left) is at the top of Bright Angel Trail.
A mule train (right) crosses a bridge over the Colorado River.

popular are Bright Angel and South Kaibab. Both start near Grand Canyon Village and drop down into the canyon. At the bottom, you can cross a long, swinging bridge high above the Colorado River.

Then follow the North
Kaibab Trail up to the
North Rim. That great hike
is 21 miles (34 kilometers)
long and can take two or
three days!

If you're big enough,
you can ride a mule down

Sure-footed mules carry visitors down the canyon trails.

Camping at the bottom of the canyon

into the canyon. At the bottom, you can swim and fish in the chilly Colorado River. You can camp down there. Or you can spend a night at Phantom Ranch.

Left: A park ranger talks
to visitors about the canyon.
Above: Phantom Ranch

Back up on the rim,
don't miss the Park
Ranger programs.
"Geology for Kids" uses
games and activities to
teach about the geology of
the Grand Canyon. Geology
is the study of the Earth's
features and history.

Another popular Park Ranger program is "Grand Canyon for Kids." You can have fun while learning about the plants and animals of Grand Canyon National Park.

And be sure to pick up a free copy of *The Young Adventurer.* This is a newspaper just for young visitors. It has puzzles and games, and it tells about things to do in the park.

The pine squirrel (left) and the mule deer (right)

WILDLIFE AT THE GRAND CANYON

There is life everywhere in the Grand Canyon. You can see hundreds of mule deer. Mule deer got that name because they have big ears like mules.

Up in the trees, look for the busy little pine squirrel.

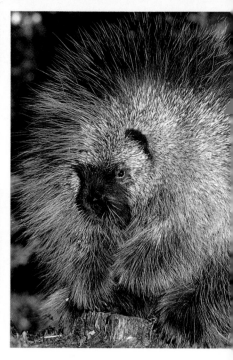

The porcupine (far right), the rock squirrel (above right), and the golden-mantled ground squirrel (bottom right)

Another animal that lives in the trees of the park is the porcupine. It has long, sharp spines, called quills. It's a walking cactus!

Scurrying around on the ground are fat rock squirrels and the little golden-mantled ground squirrel.

26

A collared lizard (top left),
elk (bottom left),
and the desert bighorn sheep
(top right)

Down in the canyon you
may see a bright collared
lizard sunbathing on a rock.
Back in the forests live
elk, a kind of big deer.
And down in the canyon
are desert bighorn sheep.

Animals that hunt and eat other animals for food are called predators.

Predators are important. They help to keep nature in balance.

The cougar is a predator that hunts bighorn sheep, elk, and deer. It is the largest wild cat north of Mexico.

The cougar or mountain lion (left) and the black bear (right)

Bobcats (left) and coyotes (right) hunt small animals.

On rare occasions an even bigger predator, the black bear, visits the park. Bears eat meat, but they also eat berries, grass, and even wildflowers.

Two smaller predators, the bobcat and the coyote, live in the park. They hunt

A raven (left) looks like a big crow. The pinyon pine (right) has delicious nuts.

squirrels, rabbits, mice, and other small animals.

One of the most entertaining creatures at the Grand Canyon is the raven. The raven enjoys watching people.

The Grand Canyon has interesting plant life, too. The bushy pinyon tree is

Juniper trees (left) and
yuccas (above) grow in the park.

one of the most common trees in the park. A neighbor of the pinyon is the shaggy-barked juniper tree.

Agave and yucca plants grow low to the ground. Both have long, sharp leaves like spear points.

31

And down in the canyon, where it's hot and dry like a desert, you'll see cactus. In the springtime, the park is decorated with beautiful wildflowers. One of the prettiest is the bright red Indian paintbrush.

The Indian paintbrush (left) and the flowering hedgehog cactus (right) decorate the park in spring.

Microbiotic soil looks like a bumpy black crust covering the ground.

The smallest living thing at the Grand Canyon has a big name. It's called microbiotic soil.

Microbiotic soil is actually a colony of tiny plants living together. It looks like a bumpy black crust on the sand. It does the important jobs of holding moisture and slowing erosion. Be careful not to step on microbiotic soil. A footprint in microbiotic soil can take fifteen years to heal!

At Grand Canyon National Park, there are 75 kinds of mammals, 50 kinds of reptiles and amphibians, 300 kinds of birds, and 25 kinds of fish.

The Anasazi drew pictures on the canyon walls.

HUMAN LIFE AT THE GRAND CANYON

Native Americans have known about the Grand Canyon for thousands of years. And they have always made good use of the wild plants and animals living there.

The American Indians make a sudsy soap from yucca roots. The big red buds of the prickly pear cactus are sweet like candy.

The shaggy bark of the juniper tree can be woven into baskets and sandals. The

Pinyon nuts grow inside cones (above); the red buds of the prickly pear cactus (below right); an Anasazi sandal (below)

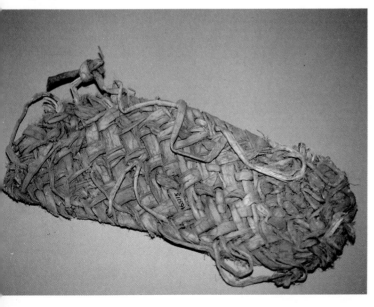

pinyon pine has delicious nuts. And many wild creatures are good to eat.

Some of the earliest people living at the Grand Canyon were the Anasazi. *Anasazi* is a Navajo word meaning "the ancient ones."

At first, the Anasazi hunted, fished, gathered wild plants, and wove baskets. Since they moved around a lot, they made simple houses out of brush.

An Anasazi basket (left) holds corn and squash. The Anasazi made these needles out of bone (right).

Later, the Anasazi settled down and became farmers. They grew corn, beans, and squash. And they learned to build strong houses of stone and mud.

You can explore the ruins of an Anasazi village at Tusayan, near the park's

The ruins of Anasazi houses at Tusayan

east entrance. While there, you can visit the museum to learn more about these early Native Americans.

A few miles from Tusayan, at Desert View, is the

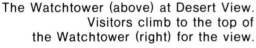
The Watchtower (above) at Desert View.
Visitors climb to the top of
the Watchtower (right) for the view.

Watchtower. This stone tower is 70 feet (21 meters) tall. Climb the winding stairs all the way to the top. From there, you can see for miles down the twisting canyon.

On the Navajo Reservation, modern and traditional houses are found. Navajo elders keep the customs of their people alive.

Many Native Americans still live near Grand Canyon National Park. The Navajo Reservation joins the park on its northeast border. And down in the bottom of the canyon is

41

Havasupai means "People of the Blue-Green Water." These Native Americans have lived at the Grand Canyon for hundreds of years.

Supai Village, home of the Havasupai people.

The Hualapai Reservation borders the South Rim just west of Grand Canyon Village.

42

PLAN TO STAY AWHILE

There is so much to see and do at the Grand Canyon.

You can hike, ride a mule, swim, camp, fish, explore, and take pictures.

Havasu Falls

Visitors can go
for float trips
on the river or
ride the train.

You can ride the steam-
powered Grand Canyon
train. You can take an
exciting (and wet!) float
trip down the Colorado
River. You can even fly in
an airplane over the canyon.

There is always something new to see and do at the beautiful Grand Canyon.

Because Grand Canyon National Park is such a special place, you'll want to stay as long as possible. Many visitors to the Grand Canyon have so much fun they never want to leave!

45

WORDS YOU SHOULD KNOW

agave (uh • GAH•vay) —a short desert plant with thick, fleshy leaves

amphibian (am •FIB •ee •yin) —an animal that lives both on land and in water

Anasazi (an •ah •SAH •zee) —the people who lived in the American Southwest until about seven hundred years ago

cactus (KACK •tuss) —a plant that is found in very dry areas; it has thick leaves and stems for storing water

colony (KAHL •uh •nee) —a group of the same kind of plants that live very close together

cougar (KOO •ger) —a large cat; also called mountain lion or puma

coyote (kye •OH •tee) —an animal that looks like a small wolf

deposited (dih • PAH•zih •tid) —laid down; dropped

erosion (ih •RO •zhun) —the wearing away of the land, caused by the action of wind or water

exposed (ex •POZED) —uncovered; revealed

fossil (FAW •sil) —the hardened remains of a plant or an animal that lived long ago

geology (gee •AHL •uh •gee) —the study of the Earth's features and history

juniper tree (JOO •nih • per TREE) —a small evergreen tree that has cones like berries

mammal (MAM • il) —one of a group of warm-blooded animals that have hair and nurse their young with milk

microbiotic soil (my •kro •by •AH • tik SOYL) —a colony of tiny plants that looks like a bumpy black crust on the sand

pinyon tree (PIN • yun TREE) —a small pine tree that has nutlike seeds that are good to eat

porcupine (POR • kew • pyne) — a small mammal that is covered with sharp, needlelike spines called quills

predator (PREH • dih • ter) — an animal that kills and eats other animals

raven (RAY • vin) — a large black bird

reptile (REP • tyle) — a cold-blooded animal that has a backbone and very short legs or no legs at all

silt (SIHLT) — small particles of sand and mud

suspended (suss • PEN • did) — held up and carried along; as small pieces of dirt in water or the air

viewpoint (VYOO • point) — a place from which people can see a long way

yucca (YUCK • ah) — a green plant with long, stiff, pointed leaves

INDEX

About the Author

David Petersen teaches writing at Fort Lewis College in Durango, Colorado. A self-described "older child," he has been exploring and enjoying the Grand Canyon for more than forty years.

DEMCO